Vision for a Better Life

Overcoming Everyday Hindrances

Gary Morris

Copyright © 2016 by Gary Morris

All rights reserved. No part of this publication may be reproduced, distributed or transmitted in any form or by any means, without prior written permission.

Scripture quotations marked (ESV) are taken from The Holy Bible, English Standard Version (ESV), copyright © 2001 by Crossway Bibles, a publishing ministry of Good News Publishers. Used by permission. All rights reserved.

Scripture quotations marked (KJV) are taken from The King James Version, 1987 printing.

Scripture quotation marked (NASB) are taken from the NEW AMERICAN STANDARD BIBLE®, Copyright © 1960, 1962, 1963, 1968, 1971, 1972, 1973, 1975, 1977, 1995 by The Lockman Foundation. Used by permission.

Scripture quotations marked (NIV) are taken from the Holy Bible, New International Version. Copyright © 1973, 1978, 1984 by the International Bible Society. Used by permission of the International Bible Society.

Scripture quotations marked (NKJV) are taken from the New King James Version®. Copyright © 1982 by Thomas Nelson, Inc. Used by permission. All rights reserved.

Scripture quotations marked (NLT) are taken from the Holy Bible, New Living Translation, copyright © 1996. Used by permission of Tyndale House Publishers, Inc., Wheaton, Illinois 60189. All rights reserved.

Sermon to Book
www.sermontobook.com

Vision for a Better Life / Gary Morris
ISBN-13: 978-1-945793-04-2
ISBN-10: 1-945793-04-X

I dedicate this book to those who have stuck by me through some of the darkest days of my life and helped me hang on to a God-given vision for a better life.

Karol, you have been an inspiration, a steady source of encouragement and strength for me. Thank you for your support and prayers. I love you dearly, and I'm so honored to share my life with you.

Sheree and Lauren, thank you for loving me, praying for me, and never giving up on me, even when it looked hopeless. I love you both to the moon and back!

I dedicate "Vision for A Better Life" to my Life Church family. To all the "Dream-Teamers" who are living out the dream with me, the Intercessors who continually hold me up in prayer, and each and every one who worships with us each Sunday, giving me an opportunity to share the vision God has given me for Life Church and Meridian.

I also dedicate this book to those I have crossed paths with who were homeless, helpless, and hopeless. Thank you for the opportunity to share my story with you, and to show you how God can bring an individual from rock bottom to a new life in Christ. Let me encourage you to keep the faith, and maintain the vision that God has given you, and let's walk into the better life together.

Finally, I would like to dedicate "Vision for A Better Life" to my friends whom I meet with weekly at Righteous Oaks Recovery Center. You guys are probably more of an inspiration to me than I am to you. Sharing my story with you and helping to develop a vision for a better life is one of the highlights of my week. Hang in there, keep the faith, and go live out the vision God has planted in your hearts. I'm excited to see where your vision will take you.

CONTENTS

A Note from the Author 7
A Golden Ticket 9
Vision for a Better Life 11
Natural Hindrances 27
Tearing Down the Walls 45
Manmade Hindrances 69
Personal Hindrances 89
This Moment Matters 111
Notes 113
About the Author 118
About SermonToBook.Com 120

A Note from the Author

Thank you for purchasing *Vision for a Better Life*.

Accompanying each main chapter of the book is a set of reflective questions and a practical, action-oriented summary. These workbook sections are a practical tool to help you find God's vision for your life and pursue this better life in obedience to Him.

I recommend you go through these workbook sections with a pen in order to write your thoughts and record notes in the areas provided. The questions are suitable for independent reflection, discussion with a friend, or review with a study group.

Regardless of how you choose to use and enjoy the book, my hope and prayer is that the experience helps you discover and grow into your vision for a better life.

INTRODUCTION

A Golden Ticket

I believe that we are living in the Last Days, that perilous times are here, and that more are coming—but I also believe that for the child of God, in the midst of these troubling times, one can maintain a vision for a better life. I'm not just talking about heaven, either. I believe there is a better life for us here, today.

According to a widely circulated news story from April 2015, a couple named Tito and Amanda were arrested in Florida for selling tickets to heaven.[1] Each ticket was sold for $99.99, and the buyers were told that these "solid gold" tickets reserved the buyer a spot in heaven. Each person would simply present their ticket at the pearly gates and be let in.

After being arrested, Tito was recorded in his police statement as having said, "I don't care what the police say, the tickets are solid gold. It was Jesus who gave them to me behind KFC and said to sell them so that I can get money to go to outer space. I met an alien named Stevie who said that if I got the cash together, he would take my wife and me on a flying saucer to a planet that's made entirely of drugs! You should arrest Jesus because He's the one who gave me the golden tickets and said to sell them."

Despite these interesting comments, you might be surprised to find that, among some drug paraphernalia and a baby alligator, police confiscated $10,000 when they arrested Tito.

The disappointing reality is that if this story had been true—it turned out to be an April Fool's Internet hoax—someone seeking a better life no doubt would have bought one of these golden tickets. However, we can rest assured that there really is a better life for us, even today. And believe me, it doesn't require a golden ticket.

CHAPTER ONE

Vision for a Better Life

> The Bible recognizes no faith that does not lead to obedience, nor does it recognize any obedience that does not spring from faith. The two are opposite sides of the same coin. — **A. W. Tozer**[2]

There are things in life that call us to a new start. Consider the end of summer, when the humidity lowers and a cool breeze comes through the windows. The thought of the coming turn of the season, the changing colors of the leaves—these create in us a desire for change, a new start. Or perhaps it's the realization that there is more to life than the mundane cycle we're currently living.

Think about the prodigal son as he sat in the pigpen, muttering to himself: "What am I doing with my life? Look at the mess that I've got myself into." As he sat in the mud and mire, he began to envision a better life, one in the comfort of his father's house. Have you found yourself in moments like these? Have you found yourself yearning for change, asking, "God, what is it that You've got in store for me? What is it that You want to do in me, in my life?" If so, you're not alone.

God brought the children of Israel out of slavery, across the Red Sea and into the wilderness, where they would continually wander, unable to put a stake in the ground, unable to say, "This is home." These people were always on the move in hope of something better: the Promised Land. Yet they were paralyzed by fear and doubt.

Can you imagine being told that a better life has been promised to your people, but because of fear and doubt, you continue to wander? Can you hear this sad conversation?

"Mom, why are we here?" asked a small boy.

"Oh, my son, it's a long story. See, we left our life of slavery in Egypt, thinking we were heading to the Promised Land. Yet we have been wandering here, endlessly."

The Israelites were yearning for a change, but found themselves in the same rut over and over. However, in the midst of all the emotion, God called a man to stand up and cast vision, the vision for a better life.

Yearning for Change

> *After the death of Moses the LORD'S servant, the LORD spoke to Joshua.* — ***Joshua 1:1 (NLT)***

Joshua was one of the men who had spied out the Promised Land, returning with the news that they would be able to take it. However, they were outnumbered by the other spies, who reported that they were like grasshoppers in the eyes of the giants of the land. Yet, here we find Joshua receiving a message from the Lord, who said, "Moses my servant is dead. Therefore the time has come" (Joshua 1:2 NLT).

At this point in Israel's history, God's people had been promised an inheritance of land. In Genesis 13:15, God said, "All the land that you see I will give to you and your offspring forever" (NIV). However, God told His people that their possession of the land depended on obedience. If they chose not to obey God's instruction, He would "scatter [them] among all nations from one end of the earth to the other" (Deuteronomy 28:64 NLT). God also told them that their obedience would impact the fruitfulness of the land while they were living in it: "If you follow my decrees and are careful to obey my commands, I will send you rain in its season, and the ground will yield its crops and the trees their fruit" (Leviticus 26:3-4 NIV). In spite of God's promises, Israel indeed disobeyed and found herself in slavery to the Egyptians.

Almost four hundred years later, God brought them out of Egypt with the renewed promise of this new land. Now, in Joshua 1, we find His people on the threshold of great new things and, yet again, at a stopping point. In this moment of fear and doubt, God says, "The time has come. Now is the time."

Today is the day to begin envisioning a better life. I believe that God has something better for all of us than what we are in the middle of right now. The day arrived for Israel—the promise of a better life after hundreds of years the nation spent under Egyptian oppression. And God reminds us, even today, that the time has come for us, too.

Joshua was told: "Therefore, the time has come for you to lead these people…across the Jordan River into the land I am giving them" (Joshua 1:2 NLT). This is the time, despite the obstacles, fear, and doubt. God, the Alpha and Omega, was leading them into the land promised to Abraham, Isaac, Jacob, and then to Moses, assuring them that no one will be able to stand against them as long as they live (Joshua 1:3-5).

There is peace in these lines that I don't want you to overlook—God promises that no one will be able to stand against His will: "For I will be with you as I was with Moses" (Joshua 1:5 NLT).

In the same way that God wanted the Israelites to possess the land, He wants you to have a better life. This day, God is offering you an opportunity to look into His vision for your life, one that no one can keep you from, for He is faithful.

Overwhelming Obedience

At this point, we know that the twelve spies, two of whom were Joshua and Caleb, had already discovered the land. We also know that it was a land of abundance, as Joshua and Caleb reported, "We went into the land to which you sent us, and it does flow with milk and honey! Here is its fruit" (Numbers 13:27 NIV).

We know that the land was lush and beautiful, exactly what the Israelites longed for in their desert wandering. We also know that the land was a precious gift from God.

With this in mind, we read God's charge to Joshua: "Be strong and courageous, for you are the one who will lead these people to possess all the land I swore to their ancestors I would give them" (Joshua 1:6 NLT). He continued: "Be strong and very courageous. Be careful to obey all of the instructions…" (Joshua 1:7 NLT).

This reminder to obey instructions might seem a bit out of context in the midst of discourse about God's free gift of land. The word 'instructions' in this verse is a reference to the law that God gave to Moses, because God was encouraging the Israelites to constantly study, meditate, and discuss His commandments (Joshua 1:7-8).

In a time when we can turn on the news and watch a forklift haul away a statue of the Ten Commandments, God calls us to be faithful to them. While others seek to change, rephrase, or pick-and-choose the commandments, we must stay faithful. Overwhelming obedience to God in the midst of His promises is crucial to a better life. God instructed Joshua not to deviate from the commandments. For in staying true, Joshua would find success—and the same is true for us.

Strong, Courageous, and Not Afraid

In verse nine, God says to Joshua, "Do not be afraid or discouraged." I think this was a warning to Joshua that there would be things out there that could really take his morale away. As you are thinking about your better life and the vision God has for it, understand that there are going to be obstacles in the way that could hinder you from seeing this vision become a reality. We must hear His command to Joshua, to be strong and courageous, to not be afraid.

We are surrounded by spiritual forces, though we can't see them. There is a real enemy out there trying to tell you that you can't have a better life and you're stuck where you are. That enemy is writing lists of excuses for you so that, because of what you have done with your life or how you were born, you will not achieve the new life. I'm asking you to envision the better life that God has for you today. Envision it, and do not be afraid or discouraged because God is for you. Be courageous, despite the obstacles that come your way. Do not be afraid and do not be discouraged, despite what the enemy is scheming.

We live in a time of overwhelming security and connectedness. We have security systems on our houses and our cars, as well as the ability to carry weapons for protection. We're constantly connected to our phones, our tablets, and our computers. Some people have the idea that these means of security and connection negate our need for security and connection with God. Yet we will all walk through places in life where nothing is able to connect or secure us *but* God. As God said to Joshua, "For the LORD your God is with you wherever you go" (Joshua 1:9 NLT). God promises to protect those who are His. The psalmist affirms this in Psalm 121:8: "The

LORD will guard your going out and your coming in from this time forth and forever" (NASB).

Let this be a comfort to you: Between the place you are seated this morning and the place that God has prepared for you, He is always present.

Fighting for Peace

Scripture tells us that shortly after he received the word from the Lord, Joshua commanded the officers of Israel to go throughout the camp and tell the people to start preparations in order to cross the Jordan River. He told them, "In three days you will cross the Jordan River and take possession of the land the LORD your God is giving you" (Joshua 1:11 NLT). What we read next can be easily overlooked, but carries an important message. Verse 12 mentions that Joshua called together the tribes of Reuben, Gad, and half of the tribe of Manasseh to tell them of the Lord's plan to give them a place of rest in the land where they were currently living.

In this very land, he told them, they would plant trees, build gardens, and enjoy life. However, Joshua explained that their inhabiting of this peaceful land would come only after having helped secure land for their fellow Israelites (Joshua 1:14-15). This would mean that some of the people in these tribes would stay to secure their current land, while those fit for battle would help secure land for the other Israelites. In others words, Joshua was calling these men to fight for the peace of their brothers.

Maybe as you read this, you've been blessed spiritually in such a way that you know you are in the will of God. When you envision a better life, you think only of heaven and spiritual things because God has made you strong and ready for battle in that way. You fight and strive, like those Joshua called to secure the land, to bring others into a better life. Or, maybe as you read this you're confronted with a deep desire for a better environment, a better life.

Know today that there are others in your life who have already gone before you and are in their territory already. To them God says, "Go and help others reach their better life." There are people in your life drawing you deeper into the will and purpose of God and a better life, so that one day you might do the same for others.

What we see here is the beautiful outworking of a community working together for the benefit of another. The writer of Hebrews said, "And let us consider how to stir up one another to love and good works, not neglecting to meet together, as is the habit of some, but encouraging one another, and all the more as you see the Day drawing near" (Hebrews 10:24-25 ESV). God has clearly designed the body of Christ to work in community—to be a group of people who selflessly spur one another on.

So many of our endeavors, though we're not quick to admit it, are selfishly motivated, but here in the book of Joshua we see a beautiful picture of selfless community. It's as if Joshua were saying, "We are not in this for ourselves! We're going to help these others possess the land and we are going to stay with them until they get it, so that they might have a better life."

However, Joshua's command is only the beginning to this beautiful picture. After reading that God told Joshua to be strong and courageous three times, we see a community of people taking after their leader: "We will do whatever you command us and we will go wherever you send us."

Let me tell you friend, the Father is cheering you on, calling you into a better life. The Holy Spirit is alongside you, Jesus is calling you on, and the Church is encouraging you with every step. I believe today that we would have many more people sitting in churches across this country if God's children would only take a moment to encourage the weak. Might we take a moment to get our minds off of ourselves and our personal problems and shift our focus to encourage those around us?

Excited, Sleepless Nights

Growing up, my family always took a vacation, usually to the mountains. Now, before you get a mind full of majestic peaks and forested valleys, this was not such a picturesque vacation! While there were beautiful sights, the trip also consisted of less-than-glamorous bologna and crackers. Nevertheless, we were always so excited to go. Daddy would say to us, "We are going to get up at three o'clock in the morning and head off to Gatlinburg." The anticipation was almost too much! We couldn't sleep. Have you ever experienced that feeling?

I imagine the Israelites felt the same way just before entering the land God had promised. Just imagine their excited, sleepless nights thinking about the better life

God had promised them. This better life looked back hundreds of years to promises made through Abraham, Isaac, and Jacob—promises of a land of peace, of plenty, and of safety.

Have you imagined your better life? Are you overwhelmed with excitement at what God has in store for you?

However, prowling around is one whose whole goal is to prevent you from participating in this "better life." Jesus said in John 10:10, "The thief cometh not, but for to steal, and to kill, and to destroy: I am come that they may have life, and that they might have it more abundantly" (KJV). We will always experience this tension between what God desires for us and the enemy's destructive efforts. Envision the abundant life that God has promised us and that Jesus Christ has secured for us. Your better life will start with believing in Jesus Christ for salvation. He, like those who went ahead to secure land for their brothers, has gone before us and secured the best life of all: eternal life. When you believe in Jesus Christ for salvation, you will be able to say, like Job, "And you will feel secure, because there is hope; you will look around and take your rest in security" (Job 11:18 ESV).

There is a familiar story about three men who were working on a stone pile at a construction site. A curious passerby asked the first worker, "What are you doing?" He tersely replied, "Chiseling stone." Hoping for a better answer, he asked the second worker, "What are you doing?" "Bringing home a paycheck." Still wondering what was going on, he asked the third man, "Sir, what are you doing?" The man dropped his sledgehammer, stood erect, and his face brightened as he waved toward the site and exclaimed, "I'm building a great cathedral!" All three men were doing the same job, but only the third man had the proper vision to make his job meaningful and to put his heart into it.

Don't miss the proper vision—*God's vision*—for you, and for a better life.

WORKBOOK

Chapter One Questions

Question: How do you think Joshua felt when God told him it was time to lead the Israelites into the Promised Land?

_____
_____
_____
_____
_____
_____
_____
_____
_____
_____
_____

Question: What does being strong and courageous in your walk with God look like?

_____
_____
_____
_____

_____
_____
_____
_____
_____
_____

Question: Are you strong and ready to help others? Or do you need others to help you fight? What can you do either to help someone else or to seek out godly help?

_____
_____
_____
_____
_____
_____
_____
_____
_____
_____

Question: Why is overwhelming obedience to God important?

_____
_____
_____
_____
_____

Action: If you are yearning for a change, but find yourself stuck in the same rut, as the Israelites were, then realize that God is offering you an opportunity to look into His vision for your life. Practice overwhelming obedience to God in the midst of His promises, for this is crucial to a better life. As believers we must be strong and courageous in the face of obstacles, and we must work together in community for the benefit of each other.

Chapter One Notes

CHAPTER TWO

Natural Hindrances

Your wives, children, and livestock may remain here in the land Moses assigned to you on the east side of the Jordan River. But your strong warriors, fully armed, must lead the other tribes across the Jordan to help them conquer their territory. Stay with them. — **Joshua 1:14 (NLT)**

Sometimes natural things become a hindrance to our envisioning our better lives. For example, the Jordan River wasn't a bad thing. In fact, it was a necessary part of life in that area. Flowing almost one hundred sixty miles from the Sea of Galilee, the Jordan was a source of water for the communities along its path as well as a source of travel. It was also the water source that flowed into the Dead Sea. The prophets Elijah and Elisha miraculously crossed the river on dry ground; the Jordan was divided to the right and to the left, and the two of them crossed over. The Syrian general Naaman was healed of leprosy after dipping himself in the Jordan seven times in 2 Kings chapter 5. Clearly, the Jordan River was an important body of water.

This was the same river where John the Baptist would baptize his followers, and even where Jesus Christ would be baptized.

However, at this particular moment in the book of Joshua, the Jordan River was hindering the people of God from seeing their vision of a better life. They were on the wrong side of the Jordan. The Israelites were on the east bank of the Jordan, about five miles north of the Dead Sea, and needed to move thousands of people to the other side.

It was the wrong season for crossing such a river. In the dry season, the Jordan is about a hundred yards wide, shallow, and easier to cross. But this was the rainy season, and during the rainy season the Jordan in this area was up to a mile wide, with deep, sticky mud and wide, marshy banks.

Joshua had previously sent spies across this river to spy out the land and the city of Jericho. It was one thing for the two spies to wade and swim across the river, but not for a group of one million or more people to cross. The options were simple: Either wait until the dry season or do the impossible.

This may be similar to obstacles in your life. Perhaps there is something in your life that you can do nothing about. At times, it may be beneficial and there may be times in the future when these hindrances could be even more beneficial. However, today it is a hindrance to you and to your vision of a better life.

Scripture is full of examples of everyday people who experienced things in their lives that became obstacles to experiencing their vision for a better life.

Paul, the Apostle, was one of those people. Paul had something in his life that was a hang-up.

> ...even though I have received such wonderful revelations from God. So to keep me from becoming proud, I was given a thorn in my flesh, a messenger from Satan to torment me and keep me from becoming proud. — **2 Corinthians 12:7 (NLT)**

Paul had just explained his visions and revelations to the Corinthians in 2 Corinthians chapter 12, but then told them about the "thorn" in the flesh that was given to him. Theologians have presented many theories of what this thorn was. Some believe Paul's thorn came in the form of Jewish persecution, because so much of the context surrounding this subject of his thorn speaks of opponents. In the Bible, thorns are used to metaphorically describe the Israelites' enemies (see Numbers 33:55), so this could be a valid "thorn." Others think that Paul was referring to his own terrible past, and the memories of persecuting those he was now sent to love and serve—the church—which may have continually haunted him and kept him humble (Acts 8:1-3; Galatians 1:13; Philippians 3:6). Some have even proposed that Paul struggled with depression or with a carnal temptation. However, it seems a physical ailment is the more likely issue for Paul. In Paul's day, health issues such as malaria, Malta fever, epilepsy, convulsive attacks, and chronic ophthalmia were not uncommon.

Whatever the issue, this hindrance in Paul's life, this "thorn," was obviously something given to him to remind him of his weaknesses and need to rely on God. He was able to learn just how strong the power of Jesus Christ was. Christ's strength is made perfect in our weaknesses.

It seems that it would be a greater miracle for God to completely remove the hindrance from existence. Wouldn't it have been a great story—to read of God erasing this issue from Paul's life? Paul begged God on three separate occasions for the thorn to be removed, but God allowed it to remain. This taught Paul how to rely on God's strength daily in dealing with a hindrance.

In spite of Paul's illness, God used him mightily for the furtherance and spread of His gospel. God's grace was enough for Paul to continue in spite of what impeded him—God's power was made perfect in Paul's weakness. In many ways, God is bringing glory through your hindrances, too, and overcoming obstacles in ways you'd never even imagine!

Ever since I can remember, I have had tremors. They have been a major hindrance in my daily life. For instance, they occur sometimes while I'm writing, while I'm wiping my forehead, while I'm preaching, and while I'm eating.

Once Karol and I met another pastor and his wife for dinner. As I was eating, I got caught chasing a chicken strip. My hand was shaking so terribly that while moving it toward my mouth I had to chase the bite with my mouth—and I noticed the pastor watching.

Holding someone's hand while praying also can be difficult. I begin to tremble, and I know they can feel it. The shaking is not the Holy Spirit and I'm not about to "cut loose." Yet these tremors have kept me humble. No matter how much good I do, I'm shaking like a leaf during those moments.

This reminds me of a time when I had just finished preaching and after the service, a lady entertained a group of church members by mocking my shaking while I was ministering. She imitated how my hands would shake while I wiped my forehead and when I would point my index finger.

Another time I was in a Chinese restaurant and attempted to carry a bowl of hot egg drop soup from the buffet to my table. My hand shook so that I spilled the hot soup on my hand, which only made me shake more. I was mortified and in no mood to eat once I finally reached the table.

Tremors have been a major "natural hindrance" in my life. However, I cannot let this shaking hinder my vision of a better life. I could hide in a corner and allow this to stop me from functioning, but this is only a minor thing compared to what it could cause me to miss. It may be subtly ironic that one of my all-time favorite songs is by Rich Mullins, who sings, "Hold me Jesus, 'cause I'm shaking like a leaf."[3]

No Collision Will Obstruct My Vision

All of this brings us to a monumental question: How do we handle natural hindrances in order to see our vision through?

Let's look again at the Jordan River. It's massive in size, rising on the slopes of Mount Hermon on the border between Syria and Lebanon and has flowed southward through northern Israel to the Sea of Galilee for thousands of years. However, in that moment when Joshua stood before the nation of Israel ready to enter the Promised Land, it was nothing more than a hindrance that was keeping Joshua and his people from moving into the land of plenty.

Now, let's look at how this hindrance was handled:

> ...giving these instructions to the people: "When you see the Levitical priests carrying the Ark of the Covenant of the LORD your God, move out from your positions and follow them. Since you have never traveled this way before, they will guide you. Stay about half a mile behind them, keeping a clear distance between you and the Ark. Make sure you don't come any closer." Then Joshua told the people, "Purify yourselves, for tomorrow the LORD will do great wonders among you." — **Joshua 3:3-5 (NLT)**

This Ark of the Covenant was a chest made out of acacia wood overlaid with gold that contained the two stone tablets of the Ten Commandments. It also included Aaron's budding rod and a pot of manna. The Ark was kept in the inner sanctum of the tabernacle in the desert and eventually in the Temple in Jerusalem.

The Ark was a symbol of the presence of God. Wherever the Ark was taken, the presence of God was there and miraculous things happened. How fitting it was for Joshua to have the Ark (the Presence of God) to lead the people into the middle of a flooded river. The only way for the Israelites to reach the other side of the river was if God led them.

If you have any desire or plans to reach the other bank, you must be led by the presence of God, too.

There's something about the presence of God that changes every situation. For the Israelites, trusting in God's presence brought them to their new home. As you face natural hindrances in your life, if you will allow the presence of God to go before you, it will make all the difference in the world. Things in your life that seem like insurmountable mountains will become tiny anthills. Financial problems will come into their proper perspective. The fear that accompanies being diagnosed with a disease will be replaced by unexplainable peace. Broken relationships will somehow begin to heal. Things you can do nothing about, He will work out for you.

I can do nothing about my tremors, but if I seek the presence of God and trust Him to get me through whatever my assignment may be, major issues will become minute.

When my moment comes to step onto the platform and play my part in the ministry of the Word, by depending on the presence of God, it is as though I have no tremor issue at all. I am never concerned about whether my hands shake or not.

Look how it all went down for Joshua and his people:

> So the people left their camp to cross the Jordan, and the priests who were carrying the Ark of the Covenant went ahead of them. It was the harvest season, and the Jordan was overflowing its banks. But as soon as the feet of the priests who were carrying the Ark touched the water at the river's edge, the water above that point began backing up a great distance away at a town called Adam, which is near

> Zarethan. And the water below that point flowed on to the Dead Sea until the riverbed was dry. Then all the people crossed over near the town of Jericho. Meanwhile, the priests who were carrying the Ark of the LORD's Covenant stood on dry ground in the middle of the riverbed as the people passed by. They waited there until the whole nation of Israel had crossed the Jordan on dry ground. — ***Joshua 3:14-17 (NLT)***

Can you imagine? Those carrying the Ark of the Covenant (the very presence of God) stood on dry ground in the middle of the flooded Jordan River! Have you ever seen a flooded river? There are no dry spots anywhere around! On top of that, at the time of year the conquest took place, the snows of Mount Hermon would have been melting. The Jordan River would have been overflowing its banks, swollen as wide as one mile in places. Yet a miracle had taken place before the eyes of the people. The people were kicking up dust in the middle of the riverbed!

People have tried to come up with logical reasons why the Jordan River may have dried up, to explain away the miracle. Some say a landslide took place upstream and Joshua simply took advantage of the landslide to cross over. However, this does not make sense with Joshua 3:13: "And it shall come to pass, as soon as the soles of the feet of the priests that bear the ark of the LORD, the LORD of all the earth, shall rest in the waters of Jordan, that the waters of Jordan shall be cut off from the waters that come down from above; and they shall stand upon an heap" (KJV). How could Joshua have known a landslide was going to take place? And if it were a landslide, why would the Canaanites later say their hearts were melting with fear upon hearing of the miracle (Joshua 2:10-11)?

Simply said, God removed the massive hindrance that was keeping the Israelites out of the Promised Land.

What would it be like to stand in the middle of the mighty Mississippi River, not bogging in the mud, but kicking the sand and watching the dust drift away? Imagine standing in the middle of your better life with all your natural hindrances being only a memory. What tremors? What thorn in the flesh?

What is this mighty Jordan River that attempts to hinder God's people from living in the land of promise? What is this enormous hindrance in your life that is bigger than anything you have ever faced—that you see no way around, over, or through? In the presence of God, it is nothing! In Him, no collision will obstruct your vision!

God will make a way through, around, or over your natural hindrances to get you to the better life He has given you a glimpse of. The words of the prophet Isaiah will ring true: "Build up, build up, prepare the way, remove every obstruction from my people's way" (Isaiah 57:14 ESV).

Able When Available

Do you remember how Jesus spoke about the mountains? He said if you have faith the size of a mustard seed, you can tell a mountain to jump into a lake—and it will do so (Matthew 17:20; Mark 11:23)!

Consider David. He was the youngest son in a family of eight boys and given the meaningless job of taking care of the family sheep. But God took this "mustard seed" kid and transformed him into a mountain-moving, giant-killing king.

Gideon was a kind of mustard seed, too. Gideon came from the smallest family of the smallest tribe of Israel. But God turned his life upside-down, transforming him into a successful military leader.

Joseph had been sold by his brothers into slavery, as told in Genesis 37. But by the end of the chapter, he was serving in Potiphar's house—a military commander and government official! Joseph was given control over everything in the house, except Potiphar's wife (Genesis 39:9). This "mustard seed" Hebrew boy ended up impacting Egyptian leadership and eventually provided a refuge for his family escaping a massive famine—the same family that had rejected him years before.

And finally, Daniel was a "mustard seed" man. He had been exiled from Israel into captivity in Babylon. As a younger man, he interpreted the Babylonian King Nebuchadnezzar's dreams, and when he was around eighty years old, Daniel was thrown into a lion's den and miraculously survived—only because God's presence was with him.

Now, let's take a look at *you*. If you are a child of God today, you certainly had mustard seed beginnings. God can take you, though you may feel insignificant, and make something great out of your life! If God can take Moses, who stuttered, and use him to bring the law of God to the world, He can use you to move mountains.

Mountains are natural things, too, like the Jordan River. They have existed for thousands of years, arrayed in beauty, and are quite beneficial. Yet if they become a hindrance, move them!

Don't you think it may be time to speak to the mountains? To tell them to take a hike? Don't you think it is time to walk down to the river and walk in like it's not even there, believing that God is going to dry it up for you?

When I walk onto the platform with the notes on my iPad and the Word in my heart, I don't let my tremors get in the way. Sure, I could resign from my position, stay home, and think about how I would love to do what I know I'm called to do. I could hide, or keep my hands in my pocket, fearing someone might catch a glimpse of a little tremor. I could allow intimidation to hold me back from sharing this personal issue with you.

But would that please God? No. That's why I choose to dive in head first, trusting that God will part the hindrance and allow me to stand on solid ground. In doing so, I've found that what was once daunting now brings me pleasure. Even to know that I can share my natural hindrances with you is enough to keep me going. I hope it brings you courage.

The Jordan River once stood in the way of Joshua and his people. After they crossed, they could look back with a smile on their face and talk about the day they kicked up dust in the middle of Old Jordan.

Continue moving forward toward your better life. Don't slow down. Don't focus on the hindrances of nature. Walk through your Jordan, speak to your mountain, and forget the handicap that has held you back. Today is a new day. We're moving forward with a vision of a better life!

I once heard David Ring, a minister with cerebral palsy, say, "God is not looking for your ability, but your availability." Here's a guy who has a perfect excuse to sit back and complain about his disability. Instead he is overlooking his disability and focusing on his availability for God's call.

Bill Bright, an American evangelist who founded Campus Crusade for Christ, says this about hindrances:

> Facing the Philistine army, the Israelites were terrified and demoralized as each day, the giant Goliath hurled insults at them and their God. He challenged them to find a champion who would fight him—winner take all. No one dared to confront Goliath. But then David, a small shepherd boy, stepped forward. He would fight Goliath in the name of Jehovah-Sabaoth, the Lord of Hosts. David was confident that his Lord of Hosts would conquer the giant and deliver Israel from the Philistines. He shot a stone from his sling and Goliath came crashing down. Jehovah-Sabaoth also comes to our aid when we are in a personal crisis.
>
> For years, Hannah had been ridiculed for being barren. She pleaded with Jehovah-Sabaoth to give her a child, and the prophet Samuel was born (1 Sam. 1). Jehovah-Sabaoth still answers the cries of those who are hopelessly overpowered by foes or circumstances. He is the great Protector, Deliverer, and Enforcer of Justice. Whatever crisis you may be experiencing, cry out to Jehovah-Sabaoth, who can deliver you. He gives more grace when the burdens grow greater.[4]

God is not looking for you to overcome challenges on your own. He wants you to come to Him and trust Him to help you. He will make you able when you make yourself available. He just wants you to show up and be ready for a miracle. Your miracle! Just show up; He'll take care of the rest. Don't whine when He starts to move. Show up! Be ready! Watch God move your natural hindrances out of your way.

WORKBOOK

Chapter Two Questions

Question: How have you seen God work miracles in your life or the lives of others you know?

_____
_____
_____
_____
_____
_____
_____
_____
_____
_____
_____

Question: How do you think the Israelites felt as they stood on the riverbank? Have you ever felt the same way? Explain.

_____
_____
_____
_____

Question: Why does God sometimes give you a thorn in the flesh? How can this grow your relationship with Him?

Question: How can you ensure that you are led by the presence of God in all you do?

_____
_____
_____
_____
_____
_____

Action: Like Paul, learn how to rely on God's strength daily in dealing with the thorns in your life. Allow the presence of God to go before you, for it will make all the difference in the world. If you trust in Him, God will make a way through, around, or over your natural hindrances to get you to the better life He has in store for you.

Chapter Two Notes

CHAPTER THREE

Tearing Down the Walls

He sends more strength when the labors increase,
To added affliction He addeth His mercy,
To multiplied trials, His multiplied peace.

— **Annie Johnson Flint**[5]

I believe that God is calling us to envision something better for our lives, something bigger than we've ever imagined. God is calling you to something greater, something that your current circumstances, habits, and struggles with sin could never keep you from.

It is possible that we may envision something different for ourselves than what God has intended for us. In fact, I believe some of us have even hijacked the vision God has for our lives with excuses, limitations, and complications. In other words, we've started to doubt that God is really in charge.

Perhaps God put a larger-than-life vision in your mind. And though that vision is great and wonderful, the temptation to write it off as impossible has crept in. Excuses, like walls, stand all around—excuses about your ability, funds, and natural limitations flow while you're stuck envisioning something altogether different than what God has planned for you.

In the previous chapter, we considered natural hindrances as we examined the children of Israel victoriously crossing the Jordan River in God's care. In much the same way, I believe that God wants to carry us into the vision that he has for his Church, a vision bigger than we could ever imagine. Yet so often we find ourselves taking charge of his vision for us, doubting his ability and becoming paralyzed with fear.

In Ephesians 3:20, Paul writes:

> *Now all glory to God, who is able, through his mighty power at work within us, to accomplish infinitely more than we might ask or think.* — ***Ephesians 3:20 (NLT)***

This tells me that the God working inside of me is greater than I am; that His vision, His plan, and His ability are greater than anything that I have of my own; and that He can do infinitely more than I can ever dream of. And it could very well be that God has something greater planned than what you have ever comprehended.

So as we move forward, put your personal vision on hold and sit in the overwhelming plan that God has for us. Let's put our personal visions on hold as we begin to tear down the walls we've built that are keeping us from God's vision for our lives.

The Commander of the Lord's Army

The hindrances Joshua and the children of Israel faced were monumental. Let's begin where we last left off. Israel had just crossed the Jordan only to be confronted with yet another hindrance. They entered the land of their inheritance to come upon a massive city surrounded by walls: Jericho.

At this time in history, Jericho was a heavily fortified city amid a vast forest of palm trees in the Jordan plain, about five miles west of Jordan (Joshua 2:5, 15). The walls keeping Israel out were strong, making it the strongest fortress in all of Canaan (Numbers 22:1, 34:15). It was the Jordan River that Israel had just crossed as they entered into freedom. An embankment around the city meant the Israelite fighters had to charge upward into the city (Joshua 6:20) to take it over.

You can almost hear the murmur of the Israelites as they whispered to one another, "It didn't look quite so big on the other side of the Jordan River!" And, "The spies tried to tell us what it looked like, how big the city was. But we just never imagined it looked quite like this!" They probably second-guessed why they had even crossed the river, and likely forgot how God had just performed a miracle in bringing them to that point.

Hindrances prevent us from seeing what God wants for us and what God wants to do in us. In the midst of hindrances, we must never forget where we've come from and who brought us through.

Up to this point, the children of Israel had come through the Jordan River, had put their stones there as a memorial, and were gazing at the city of Jericho. Joshua 5:13 explains that as Joshua neared the city, he looked and saw a man standing in front of him with a sword in his hand. Joshua was not expecting this. He was sizing up the walls of the city, brainstorming different ways to lead the children of Israel to conquer this place, only to look up and see an armed man before him. Imagine his concern!

Gathering himself in courage, Joshua approached the man and asked, "Are you friend or foe?" (Joshua 5:13 NLT). The King James Version puts it like this: "Art thou for us, or for our adversaries?" To our surprise, Joshua was met with a confusing answer: "'Neither one,' he replied, 'I am the commander of the LORD's army'" (Joshua 5:14 NLT).

Here stood Joshua, the general of the army of Israel, wanting to take this city; but before he could move, he had to confront this man with a sword, who stood between him and Jericho. Joshua was face to face with the Captain of the Lord's hosts, the Commander of the Lord's armies—the Warrior and Leader—who was not coming to help, but to take charge.

The Captain of the Lord's hosts came not only to direct the armies of Israel, but also to fight for Israel, with Israel, and through Israel. This is the same truth as is taught in Ephesians 6:10, in which Paul exhorted believers to "be strong in the Lord, and in the strength of His might" (NASB).

If the Commander of the Lord's army was standing before Joshua, where was the Lord's army? Recall here the scriptures in which we see and hear of angelic beings or angelic hosts.

For instance, as recounted in 2 Kings 6:17, Elisha and the Israelites were about to go to battle against the powerful Syrians. However, upon arising in the morning, Elisha saw the vast army ready to tear them apart. Elisha's servant who saw this army was naturally afraid, saying, "What shall we do?" (2 Kings 6:15 ESV). He knew there was little to no chance they would escape alive. However, Elisha the prophet prayed, "O LORD, Open his eyes and let him see!" (2 Kings 6:17 NLT)

Elisha replied, "Do not be afraid, for those who are with us are more than those who are with them" (2 Kings 6:16 ESV). The servant's eyes were opened, and at that moment, he saw the great angelic army of the Lord, the reality that he could not see before. There were more with him and Elisha than those assembled against them—so many they could not be counted. And before Joshua stood the Commander of the Lord's army.

Now, we must take a moment to recognize the powerful lesson here. Joshua could have replied, "But I am the commander! This is my job and my army—this is my battle." After all, God called Joshua to lead the children of Israel, to spy out the land where they now stood, and to guide these people! Yet, what do you suppose the Commander would have thought of such protests?

You see, we so often get wrapped up in arguing over our job, our role, our position, or what we believe God wants us to do, that we often miss the reality—the greater vision for our lives that God has placed right in front of us. Yet as Joshua heard this man reveal his title, he fell with his face to the ground in reverence and submission.

It is interesting to note that for the majority of church history, theologians and scholars believed the Commander of the Lord's army mentioned here was, and is, the pre-incarnate Jesus Christ. An angel, according to Scripture, will not allow man to worship him. We do not worship angelic beings, for they are created beings and we are to worship the Creator. With that in mind, looking to this Scripture, we see Joshua falling with his face to the ground in reverence. It is from this posture that Joshua said, "I am at your command..." (Joshua 5:14 NLT).

Let that powerful image sink in! Notice the change in his attitude. Here was Joshua, the strong and courageous leader of the children of Israel, kneeling before this man and saying, "I am at your command." Joshua fell on his face in reverence, in worship, and said, "I am at your command." And then he asked, "What do you want your servant to do?" (Joshua 5:14 NLT).

Joshua's initial questions were those of authority: "Who are you? Are you on our side or are you on God's side?" Yet we see that his response was one of overwhelming humility, flat on the ground in reverence. He worshiped. He submitted. He asked for guidance.

Israel had reached a point in their invasion plans when they also needed supernatural help. Jericho was surrounded by impregnable, fortified walls and defended by a well-trained enemy military. Both were seemingly insurmountable obstacles.

Yet as Joshua stood near Jericho, likely trying to figure out what in the world he was going to do next, the Commander of the Lord's army appeared to him. Joshua fell down before Him and said, "Tell me what you want me to do."

Joshua had been confronted with a situation in which God yet again expanded the vision Joshua had for himself and for the people.

Spinning Our Wheels

When we began discussing a vision of a better life, you may have envisioned life on a cruise ship or life in the Bahamas. Joshua himself had envisioned something great: conquering the land with his own power! He had even begun to plan and strategize how he would go about doing it. But, do you think it's possible that, much like Joshua, you've hijacked God's vision for your life with your own plans, limitations, excuses, or strategies? Do you think it's possible that God has come up with something far bigger than you could ever envision?

In these moments, we must stop, submit to God, and surrender what we think His vision is for our lives, allowing Him to work powerfully through us. Jesus says in John 14:12: "Truly, truly, I say to you, whoever believes in me will also do the works that I do; and greater works than these will he do…" (ESV). When we remember what God has done in the past and believe Him for what is ahead, He will do amazing things through us, "for it is God who works in you to will and to act in order to fulfill his good purpose" (Philippians 2:13 NIV).

Joshua had a vision and a plan, but standing face-to-face with the Commander of the Lord's army, he could only submit and surrender, asking, "What do you want me to do?" Maybe this is where you find yourself as you read. What we're learning here is simple: You are not in charge of your vision. I am not in charge of my vision. God is. If we continue to force our own visions into reality, pursuing our own plans without surrendering those to God in exchange for what He has for us, we will do nothing more than spin our wheels.

As we stand, like Joshua, in the presence of God every day, we must remember that we will never be able to live the vision that He has for us until we allow Him to carry us to where He wants us to be.

Strength to Surrender

He must become greater; I must become less. — ***John 3:30 (NIV)***

In the eyes of the world, that sounds weak, it sounds weak to kneel before someone and ask what they want you to do. In the eyes of the world, a strong and courageous man falling on his face and asking this sounds like cowardice. Yet I believe it is an image of immense strength.

Now, many of us would expect this Commander of the Lord's army to give a clear and mighty command, casting a lofty vision for the Israelites to secure victory. In fact, this idea is a reflection of what I personally want from God when I ask for guidance, instruction, and direction. I want God to spell it out, to send me an email, to write in the clouds exactly what He wants me to do and how I can be most successful. Can you relate?

But here we find Joshua, the strong one ready to take Jericho, the courageous one ready to take this Promised Land for his people, lying on the floor and saying, "What do you want me to do?" It is here that God expands our understanding of strength and courage, for Joshua had the courage and the strength to surrender his plan in exchange for the Lord's.

As we read of Joshua kneeling and the suspense builds, we eagerly await this mysterious man's answer to Joshua's question. What great things did this Commander ask Joshua to do? In the concluding verse of this chapter, we find the Commander of the Lord's army, standing sword in hand with the angelic hosts around him, commanding Joshua, "Take off your sandals, for the place where you are standing is holy" (Joshua 5:15 NLT).

This command reinforces the idea that we need to give up trying to do things on our own. Your strength will never be enough. God wants you to relinquish your own limited strength for His power. Paul reminds us in 2 Corinthians 12:10 that we are only strong when we are weak. Whatever you give up, God will replace with something far better.

In fact, God frequently places us in positions where we struggle and feel weak. He does this so that He receives particular glory by showing His strength through our weaknesses. We want all glory to go to God, and to do that we must boast in our own weaknesses. This way, "the power of Christ may rest upon me" (2 Corinthians 12:9 ESV). We want God to get the glory, and to give it to Him we must boast in our weakness, just as Paul declared in 2 Corinthians 12:10 (NIV): "That is why, for Christ's sake, I delight in weaknesses, in insults, in hardships, in persecutions, in difficulties. For when I am weak, then I am strong."

Ask yourself the following questions:

- Do I exhibit a life of surrender daily? How?
- What hinders my ability to surrender to God?
- What would allow God to work and be exhibited in and through me?
- How can I initiate surrender and discipline myself to carry it out?
- What can I do to arrive at the point of surrender better, stronger, and faster, even in times of uncertainty and stress?

Dr. Richard J. Krejcir says this about surrender:

> The Discipline of Surrender means we trust our Lord Jesus Christ in all things without doubt or fault in our faith. We let go our hold on our perceived rights, agendas, and opinions that are not lined up to His. In this way, we can surrender to His love and embrace God's will for our lives, live His Way in holiness, and become a benefit to the lives of others. We come before God and under new management—His.[6]

Sometimes in the church, surrender is used interchangeably with the words 'submission' and 'obedience.' Each reflects the ultimate battle in our life, which is not with arms; it is with our wills—we must deny pride and selfish motives and instead follow the One who knows us and has a plan for us, regardless of the cost.

Forget the Pressure, Enjoy the Presence

If we're honest, we might confess how disappointing and even confusing God's command to Joshua is in light of all that we've read so far. However, once again, God was after so much more than we expect or readily comprehend. In essence, the Commander told Joshua, "Forget the pressure and enjoy the presence. Forget for a moment the pressure of capturing Jericho; forget the weight of leading Israel; forget this army you are leading; forget all of these people waiting on you; forget all of the pressure. Simply enjoy the presence of God."

How much time did you spend this past week enjoying God's presence? Have you frantically rushed around town, dropping your kids at their sports activities or friends' houses? Was your calendar packed with meetings and appointments? Was your phone wooing you with text messages that seem to need immediate answers? Were you frantically trying to respond to emails? Or did your work schedule require you to come in early and leave late?

These are normal day-to-day activities. The question is, did you settle into God's presence *while you did them?* Most of us find ourselves too busy to be still and wait on the Lord; we forge through with our list of to-dos and forget about the Commander of Angel Armies who is waiting to help us in the middle of the craziness. This is where Joshua arrived: The battle was not going to stop, and he could either continue to fight on his own (and likely be clobbered) or submit to the Lord and let Him fight the battle for him.

I want to tell you as you read this today: Forget the pressure of your vision, or what it's going to look like in the days to come, and experience the presence of God. I often get so carried away and so wrapped up in the pressure, asking "God, how are we going to do this or that?" Yet here I'm reminded that in the midst of all of the hustle and bustle that comes with seeing a vision come to reality, God is calling us to enjoy His marvelous presence.

In the presence of the Commander of the Lord's army, Joshua obeyed. We must realize that someone greater than us is in charge of this venture, this vision for a better life, and this Greater One is worthy of our obedience. Forget the pressure and enjoy the presence!

The famous theologian A. W. Tozer says it well: "The reason why many are still troubled, still seeking, still making little forward progress is because they haven't yet come to the end of themselves. We're still trying to give orders, and interfering with God's work within us."[7]

How many of us are still trying to "give orders" and "interfere with God's work within us"? It's time to lay our swords down and ask of the Lord, "What do You want me to do?"

What Their Faith Requires

People tend to think that God is unknowable because He is so big and vast, and that He may even hide Himself from His creation. This could not be further from the truth, however. God does reveal Himself—through creation, through history, through Jesus, and ultimately through the pages of the Bible.

Think about this: Christ will be to His people what their faith requires.

There are many people who look at the sun, moon, and stars—the beauty of the natural world—and conclude that there is a God who at least exists. Paul talked about how God reveals Himself in this way, saying, "For since the creation of the world God's invisible qualities—his eternal power and divine nature—have been clearly seen, being understood from what has been made, so that people are without excuse" (Romans 1:20 NIV). The heavens are what made King David stand in awe at his Creator: "When I look at your heavens, the work of your fingers, the moon and the stars, which you have set in place, what is man that you are mindful of him, and the son of man that you care for him?" (Psalm 8:3-4 ESV).

God also reveals Himself through history. Skeptics are notorious for asking God to reveal Himself to the world, if He is actually real. They make the assumption, wrongly of course, that God hasn't already done it. God has spoken through the written Word of God, and through the Word has revealed things that were going to happen—often hundreds if not thousands of years before they would happen. For example, God spoke through the prophet Micah, foretelling the actual birthplace of the Messiah seven hundred years before the birth of Christ: "But you, Bethlehem Ephrathah, though you are small among the clans of Judah, out of you will come for me one who will be ruler over Israel, whose origins are from of old, from ancient times" (Micah 5:2 NIV). Lo and behold, Jesus our Messiah was born in Bethlehem, just as God said! How much more obvious can God be in revealing Himself?

God revealed Himself through Jesus, who is the exact representation of the Father (Hebrews 1:3 NIV). Paul wrote, "The Son [Jesus] is the image of the invisible God, the firstborn over all creation" (Colossians 1:15 NIV).

Though Jesus set aside the prerogatives of divinity, He clearly taught that anyone who saw Him saw God the Father. Consider the following verses:

*Jesus answered: "...Anyone who has seen me has seen the Father." — **John 14:9 (NIV)***

*By myself I can do nothing; I judge only as I hear, and my judgment is just, for I seek not to please myself but him who sent me. — **John 5:30 (NIV)***

*...I do nothing on my own but speak just what the Father has taught me. — **John 8:28 (NIV)***

Jesus revealed God's character in all He did and taught; in dying and being raised from the dead, He revealed to humanity God's plan of how He was going to rectify the issue of sin. He thereby revealed the glorious destiny God has promised to His people.

God made Himself known to people throughout the Bible, in very personal and often tangible ways. God appeared to Joshua, a strong and courageous general, as the Commander of the Lord's army. To Abraham, the traveler, God appeared as a traveler. The great wrestler of life, Jacob, met Him in a wrestling match. To Moses, the shepherd, God appeared in a fire, drawing Moses to Him much as Moses's light drew in the sheep. Paul, the bright and intelligent, was blinded by the overwhelming presence of God.

Adam and Eve chose to sin against God in the Garden of Eden, but God did not abandon them. Instead, He met them in their distraught condition in the garden, in the cool of the evening, saying, "Where are you?" (Genesis 3:8-9).

When David was running away from Saul, fleeing for his life, God protected him. Saul searched for him day after day while David hid in the hills of the Desert of Ziph, but "God did not give David into his hands" (1 Samuel 23:14 NIV).

Sometimes, to get people's attention, God will even reveal Himself in dreams and visions. For example, God spoke to Joseph the father of Jesus in a dream, in grace and love, telling Joseph to take Jesus and Mary and flee to Egypt to avoid Herod's wrath.

I don't know what you need this day or where it is that you find yourself, but God is uniquely revealing Himself to you so that you might see Him. Don't miss Him.

An Unexpected Path

Around 2011, my wife Karol and I began praying that God would prepare us for whatever He had in store for us. At that time, our vision didn't include ministry. I said, "I'm not going to pastor, and I am not going to preach. I'm not going to do anything like that!" And we started praying day and night for His guidance, for His vision. We began to hunger for something new because we were tired of where we were.

On February 26, 2012, I wrote a journal entry describing a moment that would come to change the course of our lives. This was only three or four months after we had started attending Life Church. As on most Sundays, I came to church that morning, worshiped, heard the preaching, prayed, and went home. Karol went upstairs to take a nap, and I took to YouTube and listened to Francis Chan teach. I carried the dogs into the backyard, and as they played, I sat on the swing, weeping.

This is what I wrote:

Sunday afternoon, February 26, 2012:

After listening to Francis Chan, I took the dogs out and I spent time pouring my heart out to God as I sat on the swing. I confessed a lot of things and gave up a lot of things that I had held deep inside. As I was praying, I felt as though God spoke to me and let me know that I would never speak again in the same places that I had spoken before, but the places that God would lead me to speak would surprise me. Someday, and I feel soon, the doors will open and I will have the opportunity to touch lives through speaking again. Today I am just allowing the Holy Spirit to prepare me for what He opens. It's all in God's hands. God, if you can use anything, you can use me.

I'm asking you today, "Where are you?" On February 26, 2012, we were praying, "God prepare us. Make us ready. We will do anything, but we're not doing *that*." Yet exactly twelve months to the day was Pastor Shawn Barber's last Sunday at this church, and the following Sunday was my installation as pastor of Life Church. I could never have dreamed up that plan. Only God could have.

Henry Blackaby wrote in his Bible study *Experiencing God*:

> You never find God asking persons to dream up what they want to do for Him. Without doubt, the most important factor in each (biblical) situation was not what the individual wanted to do for God. The most important factor was what God was about to do.

He added:

> God reveals His purposes (His tasks) so you will know what He plans to do...When God came to Noah He did not ask, "What do you want to do for me?" He came to reveal what He was about to do. It was far more important to know what God was about to do. It really did not matter what Noah had planned to do for God. God was about to destroy the world. He wanted to work through Noah to accomplish His purposes of saving a remnant of people and animals to repopulate the earth.[8]

Exactly a year and one week prior to my installation, God spoke to me and said, "You will not be speaking at the places where you once spoke, but you'll be surprised at where you end up."

I am still surprised.

Who's in Charge?

> We must be ready to allow ourselves to be interrupted by God. — **Dietrich Bonhoeffer**[9]

If you are where I was in 2011, telling God exactly what He can or can't do, you've put limitations on the vision that God has for you. You have hijacked it, you have doubted it, and you're trying to lead it another way. But there is hope for you today, for you've come face-to-face with the Commander of the Lord's army, with the one who wants to show you who is in charge of your vision.

God has a plan for your life. God has a plan for His church. And that plan is bigger than we could ever envision! As we stand in his presence today, let us ask, "God, what do I do?" And as the Commander told Joshua, "Enjoy God's presence."

You see, God wants to carry you to places you never thought possible. He's preparing to do a work in your life, but He is not asking you to figure it out. God is in charge of your vision. So forget the plans for today—throw the planner out the door! Forget what the calendar says, close that app, and just enjoy the presence of God today.

Can you surrender today? Can you just worship Him this day? In the meantime, as we seek His vision and guidance, let us heed the command to Joshua: Forget the pressure, enjoy the presence.

WORKBOOK

Chapter Three Questions

Question: Why is enjoying God's presence more important than a direct answer?

_____
_____
_____
_____
_____
_____
_____
_____
_____
_____

Question: When you are seeking God for direction, do you seek God's presence more or less? Why?

_____
_____
_____
_____
_____

Question: How can you shift your focus from merely wanting an answer to savoring God's presence?

Question: What does it mean that God can accomplish more than we can ask or think? When have you experienced this in your own life?

_____

_____

_____

_____

Action: God working inside of you is greater than you are, and He can do infinitely more than you can ever dream of. Don't let hindrances prevent us from seeing what God wants for us and what He wants to do in us. We must stop, submit to God, and surrender what we think His vision is for our lives, allowing Him to work powerfully through us. Forget the pressure of your vision and experience the presence of God.

Chapter Three Notes

CHAPTER FOUR

Manmade Hindrances

> The remarkable thing about God is that when you fear God, you fear nothing else, whereas if you do not fear God, you fear everything else. — **Oswald Chambers**[10]

Continuing our look into the vision for a better life that God has for us, we now turn to the manmade hindrances the keep us from that vision. Up to this point, we've been working through the book of Joshua. In doing so, we've talked about the command to be strong and courageous, the starting point of grasping God's vision for our lives. We've also discussed the natural hindrances that prevent us from a better life—in Joshua's case, it was the Jordan River. And most recently, we took a look at Joshua's confrontation once across the Jordan, revealing the ways we can hijack God's vision for our lives and the need to surrender control of that vision over to the One in charge—God. As we turn to manmade hindrances, I want to share four steps that you can take to see those manmade hindrances crumble and fall to the ground. Before we get into those steps, however, I'd like to share a story:

> There was once an older lady who lived in a peaceful community. That was until a man came to town and built a large, swanky nightclub just down the street from her home. This club was a beer joint, fit with partying, dancing, the whole nine yards! This poor old woman would lay on her bed at night and she could hear the noise, the music, the thumping all night long! She would fall on her knees and pray, "God, move that thing. Tear it down! Destroy it!" And she would pray and pray and pray and nothing would happen. Every night she could only toss and turn. Having reached her breaking point, one night this woman stayed up until the music stopped and the last car had left the parking lot. Once empty, she snuck down to the nightclub, set it afire, and moved it herself!

I can assure you, that's not an example of one of the steps I'm going to be sharing with you in this chapter! God has a much better and more freeing way for us to deal with these hindrances than to attempt to move them ourselves.

Know Your God

J. I. Packer once said, "Once you become aware that the main business you are here for is to know God, most of life's problems fall into place of their own accord."[11] How true this is!

Therefore, the first step in overcoming manmade hindrances is making sure that your Jericho knows our God. To do this, *you* must first know our God. Do you know who our God is? Do you know what our God can do? Once you know that and are confident in it, make sure that every hindrance in your life knows your God as well.

The sixth chapter of Joshua opens with this:

> *Now the gates of Jericho were tightly shut because the people who were afraid of the Israelites. No one was allowed to go out or in.* — **Joshua 6:1 (NLT)**

I want you to think about this scenario for just a moment. Here is an entire city, a whole group of people afraid of the Israelites. Why? Recall Rahab's words in Joshua 2, which were similar to Joshua 6:1. When the spies spoke with Rahab, she said, "Our hearts melted." This was because she and the people had heard what Israel's God did for them on the other side of the Jordan.

Because of the lack of mass communication like we have today, people mostly spread news by word of mouth—and inside the enclosed walls of this city, everyone was talking about the massive group of people moving toward them who had something, or Someone, on their side who was far greater than anything Jericho could come up with. The people of Jericho knew something about the God of the Israelites.

Make sure that the hindrances in your life, whatever or whomever they may be, know who your God is and what your God can do.

Perhaps you have shared your vision with your hindrance. Perhaps you have told someone what you are thinking or planning, what you believe God has shown you, and it's obvious that they doubt your vision. Maybe they're trying to convince you that your vision simply cannot happen, or maybe they've given you 101 reasons why. If this is your situation today, pause and take a deep breath. Begin to tell your hindrance what your God is all about. Begin to tell them what your God can do.

When Jesus had been teaching masses of people who were growing hungry and tired, He had compassion for them. The disciples wanted Jesus to send the people away, for it was growing late in the day. Jesus, however, did not let that hindrance stop Him. Instead, He told the disciples to give them something to eat (Matthew 14:16). Alas, there were only five loaves of bread and two fish, clearly not enough for the crowd of five thousand!

However, Jesus took the bread, broke it, and gave thanks to God, telling the disciples to distribute the food to everyone on that hillside. Scripture says, "They all ate and were satisfied, and the disciples picked up twelve basketfuls of broken pieces that were left over" (Matthew 14:20 NIV).

Is this your God? Do *others* know this is your God?

I believe my God can make dreams come true. I believe my God can bring vision to reality. I believe that my God can feed the five thousand. I believe that my God can stop a stormy sea. I believe that my God can do the impossible. I believe that my God can part the waters of the Red Sea, can bring water out of a rock, can bring manna from heaven, and can bring quail in by the thousands to care for his people. That's the God whom Jericho needs to know about.

And that's the God the people around you need to know about.

Hold On to Hope

As you share your vision, remember not to be afraid of what others will say about it. God has got something up His sleeve that He is working out in your life—for you.

I experienced firsthand the temptation to give up on the vision God had for my life. There was a point in my life when I would lie in my bed at night and try to come up with reasons not to take my life. I was at the end of the line. I had lost everything and had given up. I simply had to hold on to this hope inside of me that one day things were going to get better—that God would bring about His vision for me.

If you're in a place like I was, hold on to your hope in God! Though your life may seem to get worse all around, know that God is working something in your life, and hold on to the hope you have in Jesus Christ. You may feel like giving up, and you may feel like there is no hope at all, or no reason to try. But right now the Holy Spirit is planting a seed of hope inside of your heart. Trust that God will come through. He is faithful!

Near the old city of Jerusalem, there is a Holocaust Museum called *Yad Vashem,* dedicated to the memory of the millions of Jews who were killed by the Nazis in World War II. It has been said that going through the museum is a deeply depressing experience because you see these horrible pictures and read the accounts of the ghettos and the concentration camps. But in the midst of all the dark tales of suffering, there is one amazing story of how God can transform horror into hope.

In one of the German concentration camps, there was a young lady named Rachel. She endured great hardship from being made to work in the snow with inadequate clothing. She watched in horror as many of her friends and family members were killed. Then one day, the guards left unexpectedly. She didn't know the war was over. Later that day, some American soldiers arrived to set the prisoners free. One young American soldier told Rachel he had come to rescue her and instructed her to gather her few possessions. Then he held the door for her and said, "After you, ma'am."

Rachel started to cry. He asked, "What's wrong, ma'am?"

She said, "I can't remember the last time someone held a door open for me. It's the nicest thing anyone has done for me in a long time." The soldier stayed in touch with Rachel after she was relocated, and they became friends. Later, they fell in love and were married.[12]

That's what God can do. He can take the most terrible situation imaginable and make something beautiful out of it. Our God is an awesome God, and I'm glad He's in control. Whenever you go through tough times, you can either look for the junk or you can look for the joy. Job looked for the joy, and in the end, God rewarded Job's persistence and patience. It says in Job 42:12 (NIV) that "the LORD blessed the latter part of Job's life more than the former part."

Already Secured

The second step in overcoming manmade hindrances is never to give up on your vision. You've got a vision of a better life, of something better than what you know now, and the Holy Spirit is putting a seed of hope inside of your heart now. Don't ever give up on that vision!

In Joshua 6:2 we read: "...but the LORD said to Joshua..." (NLT). Now think about this just a moment, because we've got a problem. The mound, or "tell," of Jericho was surrounded by a great earthen rampart, or embankment, with a stone retaining wall at its base between twelve and fifteen feet high. At the top of the embankment was yet another wall, roughly forty-six meters from the base *of the retaining wall*.[13] This giant city, with its layers of virtually impregnable walls, was what the Israelites were looking up at! This Jericho was in the way of God's people getting into the Promised Land; it was a hindrance.

Yet in this simple verse, we see God taking initiative to remind Joshua that He is with him, that God's vision still stands. No matter what you may come in contact with, don't ever give up on that vision.

Whatever you focus on is where you are going to go. Think about this: When you are behind the wheel of the car, if you turn your head over your left shoulder to make sure it's okay to turn change lanes, if you aren't careful, your hands will automatically turn the wheel a tiny bit to the left. Without realizing it, you'll begin to drift left as you look left.

It's the same with vision. If you do not keep your gaze straight ahead on God's vision, if you shift your focus to any other place, you'll start to head in that direction without realizing it. And if it's not God's direction, it's the wrong direction!

As Joshua 6:2 continues, we read that the Lord said to Joshua, "I have given you Jericho" (NLT). It's as if God was saying, "Don't listen to what everyone else thinks about this vision. I've *already* given it to you!" God had already secured the victory. Maybe you've come a long way in God's vision for you and have felt fine—until you see a Jericho-sized hindrance and think, "Hmm, I wish I had never come this far." Don't ever give up on your vision, for as God said to Joshua, "I have given you Jericho, its king, and all its strong warriors." He has already secured His vision for you.

Have you ever contemplated the idea that God has already secured your future, or that the "double-retaining-wall-hindrances" in your life don't really matter because God already sees your victory on the other side? Paul wrote in 1 Corinthians 15:57, "But thanks be to God, who *gives us the victory* through our Lord Jesus Christ" (NASB, emphasis added).

Now the question becomes: How do we receive the victory already given to us?

Obedience Isn't Always Obvious

The third step in overcoming those manmade hindrances is being obedient to God. First, make sure your Jericho knows your God. Then, don't ever give up on your vision, but throughout all of this, be obedient to what God says. Stand firm. What you are doing is not in vain (1 Corinthians 15:58).

Sometimes that obedience may even look a little silly. Have you experienced this? The prophet told Naaman, who was covered with leprosy, to dip himself in the dirty Jordan River for healing. The blind man who came to Jesus said, "Speak the word and make me see." Instead, Jesus spat on the ground and made mud out of spittle and dirt, put it on his eyes, and restored his sight. Obedience isn't always obvious.

As we turn again to Joshua 6:3, we come upon a remarkable scene. "You and your fighting men should march around the town once a day for six days," God told Joshua (NLT). We've got to pause for a moment. Fighting men are trained to do what? To fight! But here God said, "You and your fighting men, start marching!" In other words, they were being asked to form a six-day parade. Again, we see that God calls us to be obedient no matter how silly it may sound.

Can you imagine their thoughts as they began marching? I imagine that the first few days weren't that big of a deal. But the fourth day, then the fifth day, I can just imagine the frustrated grumblings of the fighting men!

"Seven priests will walk ahead of the Ark, each carrying a ram's horn," God continued (Joshua 6:4 NLT). Did they have more than seven priests? Yes. So why seven? Seven is the number that God loves. Seven is the number that God works with quite often in the Bible. And why a ram's horn? The horn, or the "trumpet," was an instrument of Jubilee, an instrument of celebration; when played, it sent out the message to all of the people: "It's time to celebrate!" But it was also an instrument of warfare. It announced a coming battle. Notice what Numbers 10:9 says: "And when you go to war in your land against the adversary who oppresses you, then you shall *sound an alarm with the trumpets, that you may be remembered before the* LORD *your God, and you shall be saved from your enemies*" (ESV, emphasis added). Carrying these trumpets around the walls was a constant reminder for the Israelites of their coming victory.

God was telling Joshua that the ark on the priests' shoulders would travel around the walls of Jericho once a day for six days straight. Now, the Ark of the Covenant represented the seat of the presence of God. This detail is important because it reminds us that in all we do, we're to know that the presence of God is with us always.

Then, after six days of marching, the priests with the horns in front of the Ark of the Covenant began to blow. Then God said, "When you hear the priests give one long blast on the rams' horns, have all of the people shout out as loud as they can" (Joshua 6:5 NLT).

I know what the Israelites were thinking: "People are going to think that we are off our rockers, that we have lost our minds!" Or "People are not going to understand this. We'll look like fools!" As we mentioned before, we must be obedient to what God says, no matter how silly it may look to others. That's all that God was having Israel do—simply obey.

Are you willing to be obedient to what God says for you to do? I mean really, how badly do you want to get this manmade hindrance out of your way? Are you willing to do what God said to do in order to realize the greater vision for your life?

I would love to have been a fly on that wall when the marching finished, the horns had blown, and everyone was shouting. I would love to have seen the expression on the faces of those who were shouting as they waited to see what happened to this wall. Now, maybe you've already done your marching, or you have already been obedient to God, but you feel like it's all been in vain because nothing has come to fruition yet. Let this comfort you today: in God's timing it's all going to fall into place. God is going to honor your obedience, even if it isn't always obvious.

Songwriter and worship leader Brian Doerksen puts it this way:

> Becoming a worshiper means becoming a warrior, and by toning that down, we have sent men and women away from the church in droves. It's time to call them back as worshiping warriors. That is, as warriors who are surrendered to God, warriors who know that their authority comes because they are under authority, warriors willing to wait even when everyone else is rushing ahead, or [warriors willing to] act decisively in obedience to their commanding officer, Jesus Christ, even when everybody else is lagging behind in disobedience.[14]

I don't want to lag behind, and I certainly don't want to do so in disobedience. I want to be the one shouting the loudest and watching the walls come down.

Calling Forth the Collapse

In my study of this passage, I did some research and looked into what archaeologists have determined about the area of Jericho. It just so happens that archeologists have confirmed evidence of a great collapse of Jericho's walls. As they excavated, they found heaps of brick that had collapsed and fell into piles. This brings us to our fourth point: Watch your hindrance collapse. We read that after the Israelites were to shout, "the walls of the town will collapse, and the people can charge straight into the town" (Joshua 6:5 NLT). They obeyed and called forth, shouting out the collapse of Jericho.

First, then, you must make sure your hindrance—your Jericho—knows your God. Second, don't lose your vision. Third, in the midst of it all, be obedient to God. And fourth, watch your hindrance fall as God calls forth its collapse.

When I remember the vision that God has given me, when I remember how faithful my God is and remain obedient to Him, I know that the walls are going to collapse. Listen to Joshua's testimony: God called him out to do something ridiculous, yes, but God came through and the walls collapsed.

Vision, Faith, Obedience

Lynn Anderson tells this story of a shipload of travelers who landed on the northeast coast of America about 350 years ago:

> The first year they established a town site. The next year they elected a town government. The third year the town government planned to build a road five miles westward into the wilderness.
>
> In the fourth year the people tried to impeach their town government because they thought it was a waste of public funds to build a road five miles westward into a wilderness. Who needed to go there anyway?
>
> Here were people who had the vision to see three thousand miles across an ocean and overcome great hardships to get there. But in just a few years they were not able to see even five miles out of town. They had lost their pioneering vision.[15]

If the wall in our path blurs our vision, we may become stuck if we do not allow faith and obedience to push us through. With faith and with obedience, no ocean of difficulty is too great.

The author of Hebrews wrote, "It was by faith that the people of Israel marched around Jericho for seven days, and the walls came crashing down" (Hebrews 11:30 NLT). The New Testament refers to what happened under Joshua's leadership many years later as an encouragement to hold fast to our faith. When the wall in their path blurred their vision, the Israelites' faith and obedience carried them through.

Remember that vision, faith, and obedience result in one miraculous outcome. Do you have the vision today? Do you have the faith? Are you willing to be obedient? Those elements come together for one miraculous outcome that only God can accomplish.

You may have heard of a missionary by the name of David Livingstone. David Livingstone went to Africa and spent his life there. Yet some well-meaning men asked, "How can he call himself a missionary? He is merely a geographer. He has been discovering the watershed of a continent instead of carrying it to its thirsty inhabitants, the Water of Life." So little did they know of what was really being done. Little, perhaps, did Livingstone himself sometimes know. Through Livingstone's vision, faith, and obedience, however, the heart of the whole Church of Christ was beginning to beat for Africa.

David Livingstone walked many, many miles thinking, believing, and being obedient to God, despite looking silly to those around him. Today we see the results of his labors.

God is calling you today to do something. Sometimes God says just to be still. Sometimes God says to march. Sometimes God says to fast or to pray. Sometimes God tells us to do off-the-wall things. What is God leading you to do?

Offer the Lord your complete, unhesitating obedience and watch and wait for what He will do!

In the book *God's Smuggler*, author Brother Andrew tells the story of how he, as a young Dutch factory worker, transported Bibles across closed borders—and the miraculous ways in which God provided for him every step of the way.[16]

At one point in the book, Brother Andrew was visited by a man named Karl de Graaf, who was part of a prayer group in which people often spent hours of time in prayer, most of it listening in silence. De Graaf informed Brother Andrew that he needed to learn how to drive, even though Andrew had no reason to think he would ever need to—or even so much as own a car. Yet de Graaf simply told Brother Andrew that the Lord had given his prayer group this instruction to pass along.

Because Brother Andrew discerned that this was something God was calling him to do, he learned to drive. It seemed like a complete waste of time, an utterly illogical use of his resources, but he was obedient to the Lord's call. He pursued a driver's license.

In time, his ability to drive would prove critical for the future of his ministry, which eventually brought the gospel to thousands of people behind the Iron Curtain.

Sometimes God calls us to be obedient, even when what He's asking us to do doesn't make sense.

Through men like Joshua, Livingstone, and Brother Andrew, we're reminded of the importance of vision, obedience, and faith.

There were probably calluses on the Israelites' feet by their final march. I imagine they were sweaty and tired, but there was something about their obedience that had captured the attention of God and on that last march, at the long blast of that ram's horn, the Bible tells us that the walls of Jericho crumbled and fell to the ground.

Are you prepared for your hindrances to crumble? God is.

> To one who has faith, no explanation is necessary. To one without faith, no explanation is possible. — **Thomas Aquinas**[17]

WORKBOOK

Chapter Four Questions

Question: How did the people of Israel show faith as they marched around Jericho? What do you think was going on inside their hearts?

_____
_____
_____
_____
_____
_____
_____
_____
_____
_____
_____

Question: How did the reaction of the people of Jericho to the Israelites reflect the power of God? How can you make God bigger in your own life?

_____
_____
_____
_____

Question: How do you think Naaman felt when he was told to bathe in a dirty river? Or the blind man when Jesus used his spit to make mud to put on his eyes? In what way can you identify with their experiences?

Question: Why does God sometimes call for obedience that is not obvious?

_____
_____
_____
_____
_____
_____
_____
_____
_____

Action: The first step in overcoming manmade hindrances is to make sure your "Jericho" knows our God. The second step is never to give up on your vision, no matter what people say about it. The third step is to be obedient to God. Finally, watch your hindrance fall as God calls forth its collapse!

Chapter Four Notes

CHAPTER FIVE

Personal Hindrances

> Obstacles are those frightful things you see when you take your eyes off your goal. — **Henry Ford**[18]

An Internal Hindrance

Up to this point, we've been looking at the book of Joshua in order to better understand God's vision for a better life. What we've found as we have studied Joshua is that God is ever-present with us as we take hold of His vision for us, and that He's constantly encouraging us to be strong and courageous in doing so.

In studying the crossing of the Jordan, we've found that God is able and willing to remove the natural hindrances that block our paths. By studying Joshua's encounter with the Commander of the Lord's army, we found that in the midst of hindrances and temptations, God calls us to intentionally forget the pressures of the moment in order to enjoy His presence fully.

Through the encounter with the fortress of Jericho, we witnessed God's desire to tear down the walls of manmade hindrances in our lives. We've seen the

Israelites overcome natural hindrances (like the Jordan River) as well as manmade hindrances (like the walls of Jericho). As we further our study, we come across another hindrance—an internal one—in the way of grasping God's vision for our lives: personal hindrances.

As we begin to press on to what we have envisioned, we run into something deeper than the natural and manmade hindrances we've come across. In looking to Joshua chapter 7, we find that more often than not, we run into ourselves and are confronted with an internal battle in need of overcoming.

Joined and Knit Together

Joshua 6 ends with the walls of Jericho in rubble. Joshua and the Israelites had taken the city, destroying by sword every living thing in it—men and women, young and old, cattle, sheep, and donkeys. The chapter ends with one profound assertion that lets us know the surrounding nations were well aware of the miracle that had happened: "[Joshua's] fame spread throughout the land" (Joshua 6:27 NIV). However, there were problems already stirring for the Israelites:

> But Israel violated the instructions about the things set apart for the LORD. — ***Joshua 7:1 (NLT)***

Let's bring some context to this chapter. A man named Achan had stolen some of the items dedicated and set apart for the Lord, hiding them in the ground inside his tent, which resulted in God's anger toward the Israelites.

Israel had just witnessed their leader stand with confidence, strong and courageous, as God parted the waters at the Jordan River for them to cross on dry ground. They'd seen God working in a miraculous way as they marched around the city and the walls tumbled down, as God removed all of these hindrances from their path. The children of Israel had every reason to commit their unwavering obedience to the Lord, but here we read, "Israel violated the instructions…" (Joshua 7:1 NLT). Scripture says Achan was aware of his sin, and he knew his sin was against God alone (Joshua 7:20). Achan's personal sin was hindering not only God's vision for his life, but also His vision for the nation of Israel.

To reach your vision, to reach the fulfillment of this vision that you have, God is working out all of these things around you: the natural, the manmade—everything. Yet what if the last thing standing in your way isn't what takes place around you, but what is *inside* of you? Take a moment and ask yourself, "What am I doing to hinder what God is wanting to do in my life?" Is there something here, a personal hindrance that is preventing you from seeing your vision fulfilled?

Get Up

Let's continue on, picking up at verse ten:

But the LORD said to Joshua, "Get up!" — **Joshua 7:10 (NLT)**

The children of Israel had come from newly defeated Jericho, only to find that there was another little city called Ai standing in their way. This city had a king and an army, though much smaller than that of the Israelites.

So here was the massive Israelite army with their massive God, parting waters, tearing walls down, and doing the miraculous. They looked out and saw a little city on a hill and said, "We need to get that out of the way. But that's not going to take much, so let's send about three thousand of our soldiers to take care of this. We surely don't need to send the whole army out!" So Joshua's men did just that. They sent three thousand soldiers to little Ai, prepared to wipe them off the map, when suddenly the people of Ai came chasing after them, killing around thirty-six soldiers.

I can just hear the doubts and frustrations of the Israelites after this unexpected defeat: "You promised us a better life! You promised us land, Canaan, this place that flowed with milk and honey! You sustained us through the Jordan River and through Jericho, yet this little army has defeated us and we have lost our men!"

Yet, the Lord instructed Joshua, "Get up!" (Joshua 7:10 NLT)

Can you relate to Joshua? Have you found yourself fearing man and feeling as though God has forgotten you? The more important question is: Have you forgotten about God?

Here we find Joshua fallen to the ground, asking, "God why, why, why?" We've all been there. We have seen our Jericho walls fall and our Jordan Rivers part, yet in the midst of unexpected defeat, it is so easy to forget the power of our God. In these moments we ask, "What is happening? Where are You now, God?"

Speaking for God, the prophet Isaiah communicated this same idea. God's people had forgotten Him, and His heart was broken:

> *I, even I, am he who comforts you. Who are you that you fear mere mortals, human beings who are but grass, that you forget the* LORD *your Maker, who stretches out the heavens and who lays the foundations of the earth, that you live in constant terror every day because of the wrath of the oppressor, who is bent on destruction?* — **Isaiah 51:12-13 (NIV)**

How quickly people forget God and all of the wonderful things that He does! Here was Joshua asking those familiar questions: "Why, why, why?" And yet the Lord said to him, in short, "Get up! Why are you lying on your face like this? They have stolen some things that I commanded must be set apart for Me. Joshua, get up—you've got problems in the camp. You've got to get it straightened out before you can go any further!" (see Joshua 7:10-15).

Defeated by Distractions

Once again, let's listen to the words of Brother Andrew. He says: "I won't even consider installing one of those call waiting monstrosities that interrupt one phone conversation to announce another." Technology, Andrew says, makes us far too accessible to the demands and pressures of the moment. "Our first priority should be listening in patience and silence for the voice of God."[19]

Emails, texts, even phone calls—this generation is inundated with technology that makes life easier in some ways, but provides incredible distraction in others. There are constant demands on our attention, including social commitments and material wants and desires. Times of silence are becoming increasingly rare, if not nonexistent. People spend more and more time focusing on things that actively distract and woo them away from God's vision and plan for their life.

Israel, though great and victorious, had been brought to a point of ultimate humility. Ai was so small and insignificant compared to Jericho, yet they'd lost this battle because someone had taken something out of Jericho that God had said not to take. Someone had been led astray by distractions.

In the moments of their celebration and rejoicing, Israel had gotten distracted. Someone was distracted by something they saw but God said not to touch. Imagine the glitter of those items—the shine. Now, the items themselves were not sinful. However, because God had instructed the Israelites not to touch them, they were led into the sin of disobedience, and the consequences were great.

In verses eighteen to twenty-one, Joshua confronted Achan, who confessed that he has sinned against the Lord, the God of Israel. Among Achan's plunder, Joshua noticed a beautiful robe from Babylon, two hundred silver coins, and a bar of gold weighing more than a pound. As the celebration had continued around Jericho, the smoke still ascending over the city, Achan noticed these treasures. And although God had said not to take such items, he convinced himself that God wouldn't mind—that in the grand scheme of things, something this small wouldn't result in anything serious, and that nobody would ever know.

All of Israel was now at a standstill. God had brought them this far, and their vision of a better life was being fulfilled right before their eyes! Yet they hit the stumbling block of distraction and were consequently defeated into repentance. Achan stood before Joshua, the Israelites, and the Lord a guilty man.

There is something profound in this story that I don't want you to miss. The entire nation of Israel—all of those other soldiers ready to fight Ai, all of the women and children, all of the old men and women—had not participated in Achan's sin. But because of one man's sin, the entire nation was impacted. Don't ever discount the impact your sin can have on your family, your friendships, or even your community.

God's power had moved on Israel's behalf through that muddy Jordan River and around the towering walls of Jericho, yet now the whole country came to a standstill. Thirty-six men lost their lives and the Israelites' vision had been put on hold, all because of the glittering distractions in a city's rubble and one man's desire for them. One man deemed glimmering possessions more attractive than the presence of God, more attractive to them than the land that flows with milk and honey, more attractive than all of the provisions of God, and the entire nation paid the price. Paul put it this way: "A little yeast works through the whole batch of dough" (Galatians 5:9 NIV). Israel had been defeated by distractions.

Better Than Sacrifice

I know you've got a big vision. And I believe God has likely given you that vision and will help you see it through. Yet we must see that a better life can't be achieved when we're distracted by a myriad of internal issues, especially disobedience. Silver is not sin. Gold is not sin. Babylonian garments are not sin. The sin of Achan (and of many of us) is in the disobedience surrounding those objects.

You may be asking yourself how you can know or identify God's leading during times of temptation and trial. Yet here you must listen closely for the leading of the Holy Spirit as God speaks to your heart; listen for that still, small voice. Hear God as He speaks to you through Scripture and in prayer.

The Bible tells us that to obey is better even than a sacrifice (1 Samuel 15:22). This is important and powerful, because all through Scripture we see that sacrifice is a crucial aspect to one's relationship with God. Yet even more crucial is one's obedience to God. Obeying what God tells you and what the Holy Spirit speaks to your heart in those moments of temptation or despair matters so much to Him!

You've got a vision of a better life. God has given you a vision and you've witnessed hindrances crumble and rivers part; you have fasted, sought God, and held on to His promises. Yet, just as with Achan and the Israelites, one lingering act of disobedience, one moment of distraction, can lead a whole nation astray.

Let me tell you what I have learned as a pastor. I can't get up on the platform and preach, or sit at my desk to write about the Word of God, if I've got a lingering issue with someone in my life or an act of disobedience that hasn't been reconciled with God. First John 1:9 states, "If we confess our sin, he is faithful and just to forgive our sin and to cleanse us from all unrighteousness" (ESV). Notice the word 'if.' God offers complete reconciliation, but it hinges on 'if.' We *must* confess to God and to others any distraction—any sin—that can lead others astray.

When God speaks to your heart about something, yet you choose to go against His will, it causes problems. God wants your constant obedience even more than your sacrifice!

The pastor and founder of In Touch Ministries, Charles Stanley, says, "The bottom line in the Christian life is obedience and most people don't even like the word."[20] And yet, with obedience comes great freedom as we confess to God and He cleanses us.

Set Apart for Destruction

Have you ever had something wrong with your lawn, but couldn't figure out what it was? Perhaps you could not see where the root of the issue was, but your lawn was obviously experiencing some hidden problem. Moles will do this; they will crawl around just under the surface of a beautifully kept lawn, destroy its roots, and eventually devastate the green grass that can be seen on top—leading to a brown, ugly lawn.

The children of Israel also had a problem with a hidden issue (Joshua 7:1-26). They were experiencing difficulty but could not identify the root problem; something was concealed from their view, but that something was causing grave damage to the nation.

As we look again to the Scriptures, we read that not only did Achan steal items from the rubble, but also he lied about it and hid the trinkets among his own belongings. Hidden sin damages more than just the person committing the sin. Sin needs to be brought to the surface, or the person and those surrounding him or her will face certain defeat, as the Israelites did. That is why the Israelites were forced to run from their enemies in defeat.

And God said, "For now Israel itself has been set apart for destruction" (Joshua 7:12 NLT). The God of Abraham, Isaac, and Jacob was saying that Israel—the whole nation—had been set apart for destruction because of one man's disobedience. Achan's sin impacted all of Israel.

The effect of one person's sin on the whole was made clear to journalist Sebastian Junger. Junger was following a platoon of soldiers while covering a story. He watched one soldier accost another soldier whose bootlaces were dragging on the ground. Junger said the soldier didn't confront the other soldier out of concern for his fashion, but rather because the soldier's untied laces put the entire platoon at risk—he could trip and fall at a critical moment. The journalist realized this is what happens to a group when one person puts everyone else at risk.[21]

In a sense, Achan's "bootlaces were loose." What we learn from this story is that sin is never private. After the miraculous victory at Jericho, God was specific with Joshua on how to deal with the city and its plunder (Joshua 6:18 NASB). Scripture says the people were to "abstain from the accursed things" (John 6:18 NKJV) and to put all the silver and gold "into the treasury of the LORD" (Joshua 6:18-19 NASB). Only Achan sinned by stealing the plunder, but because of his actions, everyone was affected and God's name was defiled.

Then God declared, "I will not remain with you any longer unless you destroy the things among you that were set apart for destruction" (Joshua 7:12 NLT). It's as if God was saying, "We are not going any further with this vision because you have disobeyed Me. We are not going any further until you remove that disobedience from your life, until you get that out of your camp, and until you get to the bottom of this sin." Israel *needed* to deal with the untied laces.

Thus, the Israelites took Achan, his family, his goats, his sheep, his cattle, and everything else he had and destroyed all of them. The family was stoned and their possessions were destroyed. The children of Israel were then set free from the judgment of God and were able to defeat Ai. To continue pursuing their vision and their better life, they had to remove the internal hindrance from among them.

Sinful choices create unintended consequences. Achan's stolen and hidden booty not only cost him his life, but his family's life as well (Joshua 7:1-26). King David committed adultery with one woman, but the impact of that sin spread to his whole family—leading to much friction in his family and the entire kingdom (2 Samuel 15-18). Sin's consequences have a way of piling up—and they will eventually impact others negatively.

Do you have some issue of sin hidden in your life that needs to be "removed from the camp"? When we confess our sins to God, He promises to forgive and cleanse us (1 John 1:9). For those we have hurt, we can seek ways of righting wrongs through restitution (Luke 19:1-8). The God of grace will give us wisdom in dealing with bad decisions from our past and help us to make good ones in the future. By confessing sin and living in the power God provides, we will fight winning battles. D. De Haan writes this about sin:

> *What shame can overwhelm the soul*
> *Because we've chosen paths of sin!*
> *But if we humbly call on God,*
> *He'll grant anew His peace within.*[22]

Doing This Differently

Today we are called to repentance for the internal hindrances that keep us from our greater life, freedom, and love. We can't hide our sin. Numbers 32:23 says that "you may be sure that your sin will find you out" (NIV).

The psalmist said, " 'I will confess my transgressions to the LORD.' And You forgave the guilt of my sin" (Psalm 32:5 NIV). Confession and repentance of sin are the key—the open door to forgiveness and freedom.

Because Jesus Christ became the sacrifice of all sacrifices, we are called not to die physically, but to die spiritually in repentance. Christ died on the cross so that we could know forgiveness, grace, and love through repentance—through the turning away from the sins of our past and the disobedience in our lives, in order to pursue a new life, one of holiness and sanctification. Repentance is choosing to do things differently. We must have the willingness and desire to move away from the traps of sin in our lives and into a life of obedience.

So, what is it that you are dreaming of? What is it that you are envisioning? Are you envisioning God doing something miraculous in your home? Let the Holy Spirit stop you today as you read, to take inventory of what you've got buried at your tent door. What is it? What's buried there, keeping your future at bay? You cannot move forward with this vision for a better life if there is sin hidden on the inside—if your personal hindrance hasn't been confronted with repentance.

Remember, you can't hide anything from God, because He sees everything! We, along with Achan, only deceive ourselves when we try to hide things from the Lord. John says in 1 John 1:8, "If we claim to be without sin, we deceive ourselves and the truth is not in us" (NIV). Pretending to be without sin will only hurt us. We underestimate the God who tore the walls of Jericho down. We underestimate the God who parted the waters of the Red Sea and the Jordan River. We underestimate the God who overcame sin and death to give us freedom! So, why are we living secretly in sin as if no one knows? God sees. Your pastor or spouse may not see or know about it, but God sees it. He knows about it.

I wonder what Achan might say if we could ask him whether that little plunder was really worth it. The silver and gold and garment—were they really worth it in the end? I wonder what Achan's wife said to him as they were being stoned. I wonder what their kids screamed out. I wonder what he thought as he sat there and looked at everything he owned being destroyed. Because he fell captive to the glimmer and shine of disobedience, a whole nation was led astray and all that was important in his life was taken away.

God will cut away the gangrene if necessary in order to cause His vision to come to pass, but many other people may be impacted in the process. In Israel's case, it led to humiliation, self-examination, prayer, faith, and finally victory. David's adultery, though terrible, was followed by confession before God. Ultimately, David was referred to in the Bible as a "man after [God's] own heart" (1 Samuel 13:14 NIV).

Even though we sin, it is important to confess sin and trust God to do the impossible. He will restore us and bring us to victory.

The Sparkle of Temptation

> Every temptation is an opportunity of our getting nearer to God. — **John Quincy Adams**[23]

I once heard the story of a young mountain climber: Early one morning, as the sun was just coming up over the horizon, a shine caught the climber's eye. He looked over to find a massive diamond hanging on the side of the mountain, untouched and waiting to be taken. In his excitement, every morning the climber worked to reach that place where the diamond was lodged. Finally, the morning came when he was close enough that he could see the glitter, the sparkle, right before his eyes. So, hanging on to the rope, he kicked out with his foot in order to grab it as he swung. As he reached out and pulled his hand in, he was surprised to find only a spider web covered with dew! There had never been a diamond there, just something sparkling because the sun was shining on it a certain way.

This story reminds me of Achan. When Achan saw the sparkle of the silver and gold and the beautiful garment, he was overwhelmed with their material worth. So, he took it and ran. However, the "sparkle of his temptation" did not live up to what he thought it was going to be.

I have to ask: Did the sparkle of *your* temptation live up to what you thought it was going to be? Did the sparkle you reached for give you everything you had hoped it would? In order to see the vision that God has given you become a reality, you've got to clean up what is buried at your tent door, the stuff you've hidden from the world. You serve a miraculous God, who is strong and willing to part waters and tear down walls in order to see His vision for your life become a reality. Don't hinder God's working in your life through your disobedience. When you see that sparkle of temptation, seek Him!

In the original Greek language, the word for 'tempted' actually means "tested." A test can be for good or for evil, depending on the one giving the test. John MacArthur says, "Temptation is an inward solicitation resulting from an outward test. Life is full of those kinds of tests." [24]

Achan was tested when the riches of the plunder called to him. Tests can be financial challenges, personal disappointments, unkindness from another person, mistreatment, injustice, or even an illness—or worse, the death of a loved one. "These are the tests that make up life," MacArthur says, "and when they go inside [to your heart] then they begin to solicit evil and they become temptations."[25]

But be encouraged! Though there will always be things that tempt us in this life, Paul wrote in 1 Corinthians 10:13, "No temptation has overtaken you but such as is common to man; and God is faithful, who will not allow you to be tempted beyond what you are able, but with the temptation will provide the way of escape also, so that you will be able to endure it" (NASB).

Paul says, "No temptation." Period. There is nothing so tempting that God will not provide you a way out of.

Even Jesus was tempted (Matthew 4:1-11). But Hebrews says Jesus is the "One who has been tempted in all things as we are, yet without sin" (Hebrews 4:15 NASB). Jesus understands our weaknesses and will help us in our time of need. Be assured: what God has in store for you is far greater than what any shiny thing in this life can promise.

Victory starts by overcoming natural, manmade, and personal hindrances. It involves confession of sin and 180-degree repentance, and then accepting forgiveness. Finally, it involves a day-by-day turning from the things that tempt us back into sin. Understand where these temptations come from and then press through any hindrance, knowing there is something better waiting on the other side.

Even as Israel, having wandered for forty years and having seen every hindrance imaginable, saw their vision become a reality, so can you.

We began this study in Joshua by dreaming God-sized dreams and working to shape our unique visions for a better life. And though we've come across, and will continue to encounter, a myriad of hindrances, I trust you now feel equipped to see God bring your vision to reality.

WORKBOOK

Chapter Five Questions

Question: How does sin destroy what God is doing?

_____
_____
_____
_____
_____
_____
_____
_____
_____
_____

Question: How does temptation lure you in? How does it leave you empty? How can you break this cycle?

_____
_____
_____
_____
_____
_____

Question: What do you need to repent to God about today?

Question: Why is obedience to God more important than sacrifice? How can you seek God for growth in obedience to Him?

_____

_____

_____

_____

Action: A better life can't be achieved when we're distracted by a myriad of internal issues, especially disobedience. Obey what God tells you and what the Holy Spirit speaks to your heart in moments of temptation or despair. Maintain the willingness and desire to move away from the traps of sin in your life. And when your obedience falls short, choose to repent—to do things differently and move into a life of obedience.

Chapter Five Notes

CONCLUSION

This Moment Matters

> The Golden Rule for understanding in spiritual matters is not intellect, but obedience. — **Oswald Chambers**[26]

As I examine my own life, I've found that I have lots of goals and dreams and visions that I seek God for. Now, Satan would love to have something inside of my life, in my heart, in my mind, in my home, or in my family that would stop me from achieving those things. Thankfully, confronting our buried temptations through Jesus Christ offers us an opportunity for repentance. We are brought to a point of asking His forgiveness: "God, I have sinned. I have disobeyed and I have done wrong. Will you forgive me?" From confession, we turn to repentance and position our lives toward Him and His path to obedience.

It doesn't matter how much wrong you've done. It doesn't matter what still haunts you from the past. What matters now is this moment. God has brought you to this moment, this opportunity to turn from the sins of your past to forgiveness and peace in Jesus Christ. God has put all of this together and He is saying:

"Here it is right before you today! What I am offering to you now is repentance, is the ability to walk in a different way and follow in obedience. That is going to bring you to your vision of a better life."

Notes

1. Arneburg, Marty. "Couple Arrested for Selling Tickets to Heaven." *Jacksonville Sun Times*. 2 April 2015. http://jacksonville.suntimes.com/jax-news/7/115/241971/best-time-sell-home-florida/
2. Tozer, A. W. *Paths to Power: Living in the Spirit's Fullness*. 1911.
3. Mullins, Rich. "Hold Me Jesus."
4. Bright, Bill. In "Jehovah Sabaoth—Lord of Hosts." *Precept Austin*. http://www.preceptaustin.org/jehovah_sabaoth_-_lord_of_hosts
5. Flint, Annie Johnson. "He Giveth More Grace." *Daily Encouragement Net*. Stephen C. and Brooksyne Weber. http://www.dailyencouragement.net/hymnstory/he_giveth_more_grace.pdf
6. Krejcir, Richard J. "The Discipline of Surrender." Bible Study Notes. *Into Thy Word*, 2007. http://70030.netministry.com/apps/articles/default.asp?articleid=35064&columnid=3803&contentonly=true
7. Tozer, A. W. In "A. W. Tozer > Quotes." *Goodreads*. Goodreads Inc. https://www.goodreads.com/author/quotes/1082290.A_W_Tozer

8. Blackaby, Henry T., Richard Blackaby, and Claude King. *Experiencing God: Knowing and Doing the Will of God* (Revised and expanded edition). B&H Books, 2008.
9. Bonhoeffer, Dietrich. *Life Together*, 1954. In "Dietrich Bonhoeffer > Quotes > Quotable Quote." *Goodreads*. Goodreads Inc. http://www.goodreads.com/quotes/400341-we-must-be-ready-to-allow-ourselves-to-be-interrupted
10. Chambers, Oswald. *Run Today's Race*. Christian Literature Crusade, 1968.
11. Packer, J. I. *Knowing God*. 1973.
12. Markes, Fred. "Better Off Dead." *Sermon Central*. 2011. http://www.sermoncentral.com/sermons/better-off-dead-fred-markes-sermon-on-trials-and-difficulties-159981.asp
13. Wood, Bryant. "The Walls of Jericho." *Answers in Genesis*. 1999. https://answersingenesis.org/archaeology/the-walls-of-jericho/
14. Doerksen, Brian. *Make Love, Make War: NOW Is the Time to Worship* (New ed.). David C. Cook, 2009.
15. Lynn Anderson "A Road 5 Miles into the Wilderness." In Sermon Illustrations. *Sermon Search*. http://www.sermonsearch.com/sermon-illustrations/6945/a-road-5-miles-into-the-wilderness/

16. Brother Andrew, John Sherrill, and Elizabeth Sherrill. *God's Smuggler* (Anniversary ed.). Chosen Books, 2001.
17. Aquinas, Thomas. In "Thomas Aquinas > Quotes > Quotable Quote." *Goodreads*. Goodreads Inc. http://www.goodreads.com/quotes/344613-to-one-who-has-faith-no-explanation-is-necessary-to
18. Ford, Henry. In "Henry Ford Quotes." *BrainyQuote*. http://www.brainyquote.com/quotes/quotes/h/henryford101486.html
19. Brother Andrew, John Sherrill, and Elizabeth Sherrill. *God's Smuggler* (Anniversary ed.). Chosen Books, 2001.
20. Stanley, Charles. In "Charles Stanley Quotes." BrainyQuote. http://www.brainyquote.com/quotes/quotes/c/charlessta451707.html
21. Junger, Sebastian. *War*. Twelve, 2010.
22. De Haan, D. In "2 Samuel Devotionals." *Precept Austin*. http://www.preceptaustin.org/2samuel_devotionals
23. Adams, John Quincy. In *AZ Quotes*. http://www.azquotes.com/quote/1043826
24. MacArthur, John. "Triumphing over Temptation." *Grace to You*. 18 October 1992. http://www.gty.org/resources/sermons/80-108/Triumphing-over-Temptation
25. *Ibid.*
26. Chambers, Oswald. In "Oswald Chambers > Quotes." *Goodreads*. Goodreads Inc.

http://www.goodreads.com/author/quotes/41469.Oswald_Chambers

About the Author

In the fall of 2005, as Hurricane Katrina plowed through the Gulf States, Gary Morris found himself in a one-bedroom apartment on the north side of a Mississippi town that was proving to be a site for his painful demise. Everything he once held dear was now gone—his family, his ministry, his financial security, and most of his friends.

Although he had grown up in a pastor's home, had become a pastor himself, and served in five different churches, Gary was now at rock bottom, underneath the weight of sin, guilt, and debt. There was no way out. His income had been greatly reduced due to the economic fallout from the hurricane. His utilities were slowly being disconnected. Every day his phone rang with bill collectors hounding him.

Each night he cried himself to sleep as some country song played in the background. Thoughts of his son's grave thirty miles away, and of his family now living under another roof just as far away, only brought more pain with every sunrise. His survival tactic was simply rereading the list of reasons why he should not take his own life.

On his birthday in April 2006, he grasped a vision of a better life. Without any lights or air conditioning, he fell across his bed and wept before God. The weight of his sin began to lift, the hope of a miracle took root, and a still, small voice spoke a verse from the Psalms to his heart: "Be still and know that I am God" (Psalms 46:10).

Gary grabbed and hung on to that promise because his entire life depended on it. Within two months, he was hired on with a large investment company. Through his new job and the local church, he met a beautiful girl who soon became his wife. Together they prayed that God would prepare them and use them for whatever he could possibly use them for.

In November 2011, Gary and Karol walked into a new church plant in Meridian. By January, every sermon in that church was about forgiveness. Every song he heard was about forgiveness. Gary could not get away from the message of forgiveness, and then he realized God was leading him through a time of pulling hatred and bitterness from his closet.

He spent nearly the entire month calling people whom he had bitterly hated. He asked every one of them for forgiveness. In the process, he forgave each and every one he spoke with. It was a time of coming clean in every area of his life.

One year later, Gary and Karol were again seeking God for guidance, but this time, they were praying about the decision to accept the call to pastor the congregation of the church in which they had been restored.

Gary now serves as pastor at Life Church Meridian, a growing life-giving congregation with a special ministry to those who have found themselves searching for a reason to live. Gary shares a life-changing message of forgiveness and hope that he has experienced firsthand, one that offers a vision of a better life. Learn more at www.garymorris.co, or email him at gary@garymorris.co.

About SermonToBook.Com

SermonToBook.com began with a simple belief: that sermons should be touching lives, *not* collecting dust. That's why we turn sermons into high-quality books that are accessible to people all over the globe.

Turning your sermon or sermon series into a book exposes more people to God's Word, better equips you for counseling, accelerates future sermon prep, adds credibility to your ministry, and even helps make ends meet during tight times.

John 21:25 tells us that the world itself couldn't contain the books that would be written about the work of Jesus Christ. Our mission is to try anyway. Because, in Heaven, there will no longer be a need for sermons or books. Our time is now.

If God so leads you, we'd love to work with you on your sermon or sermon series.

Visit www.sermontobook.com to learn more.

www.ingramcontent.com/pod-product-compliance
Lightning Source LLC
Chambersburg PA
CBHW071223080426
42453CB00034B/2164